COULD YOU BE THE REFEREE?

A compilation of football referee's signals

by

Rick Yearout

authorHOUSE®

AuthorHouse™
1663 Liberty Drive, Suite 200
Bloomington, IN 47403
www.authorhouse.com
Phone: 1-800-839-8640

First published by AuthorHouse 5/28/2008

ISBN: 978-1-4343-7340-3 (e)
ISBN: 978-1-4343-7339-7 (sc)

Printed in the United States of America
Bloomington, Indiana

This book is printed on acid-free paper.

HOW THIS BOOK IS SET UP

We have assembled this easy to follow set of signals, descriptions of calls, and when required, the penalty applied. Whether you are a seasoned veteran, a coach, a die-hard fan or a newbie to the hard-hitting, smash-mouth game of football, you will be challenged by this book. After you referee your way through every page you can be assured when you see the line judge scurry out on the field and pow-wow with the head referee, there should be no doubt in your mind he made the right call or is a complete idiot.

It's time to get pumped up and discover your skill level of the game.

Once you have answered the first half 'MAKE THE CALL!', and announced the penalty when applicable, just move to the second half and reverse the process by announcing the 'call' and penalty and then demonstrate the correct signal. What an entertaining way to learn with your friends and family by making a game of it!

Acknowledgements

Thanks to Ruth Yearout, my wonderful wife, supporter and idea person credited with the award for the idea of this book, and to our daughter Amy Kay for providing grammar review, guidance and encouragement.

Could you be the referee?

What exactly does it mean when the head referee chops his forearm, strikes both hands on the sides of his thighs and marches off penalty yards against your team?

Finally available in print, a book and a game which lays out the true meaning of the bizarre gyrations seen on green and white football fields as the men in black and white blow whistles, wave, swing, point and penalize players on the field for reasons which leave so many of us bewildered.

We observe their signaling antics followed by a mysterious meeting as they huddle together to decipher why the back judge made one call and the side judge made a completely different call.

Then one of them stands in front of 70,000 fans, coaches, teams and team owners to provide some explanation why there were two yellow handkerchiefs laying out on the grass.

So you think you know the game of football WAY better than the average fan?

Do you consider yourself the authority and football "aficionado" at the office and at home?

Here is the chance you have been waiting for, ... to prove to your friends and family you know the game better than they do.

Or is it just the chance to prove to yourself you know the game as well as you thought you did?

FIRST HALF

Are you ready to take the referee's challenge?

Score (1) point for every correct call and (1) point for every correct penalty.

Let's start the first half by turning the page.

Now, MAKE THE CALL!

The referee's challenge rating system is on page 87.

MAKE THE CALL!
Penalty?

Crowd noise, dead ball or neutral zone established

5 yds.

One arm above head with an open hand.

MAKE THE CALL!
Penalty?

Delay of game, excess time out

5 yds

Folded arms.

MAKE THE CALL!
Penalty?

Facemask Incidental grasping
5 yds./automatic first down

Intentional grabbing
15 yds./automatic first down

Grasping facemask with
one hand.

MAKE THE CALL!
Penalty?

False start, illegal formation, kick out of bounds/team player out of bounds

5 yds.

Forearms rotated over/over in front of body.

MAKE THE CALL!
Penalty?

Ball illegally touched,
kicked or batted.

10 yds.

Fingertips tap both shoulders.

MAKE THE CALL!
Penalty?

Time out

Hands crisscrossed above head.

MAKE THE CALL!
Penalty?

No timeout, time in w/whistle

Full arm circled to simulate moving clock.

MAKE THE CALL!
Penalty?

First down

Arm pointed toward defensive team's goal.

MAKE THE CALL!
Penalty?

Touching a forward pass or
scrimmage kick

10 yds.

Diagonal motion of one hand
across another.

MAKE THE CALL!
Penalty?

Holding

10 yds.

Grasping one wrist, the fist clenched in front of chest.

MAKE THE CALL!
Penalty?

Illegal shift

5 yds.

Horizontal arcs with two hands.

MAKE THE CALL!
Penalty?

Illegal use of hands, arms or body

10 yds.

Grasping one wrist, the hand open and facing forward in front of chest.

MAKE THE CALL!
Penalty?

Penalty refused, incomplete pass, missed field goal, extra point or play over

Scissors arms action in front of chest.

MAKE THE CALL!
Penalty?

Pass juggled inbounds/caught out of bounds

Hands up and down in front of chest.

MAKE THE CALL!
Penalty?

Illegal forward pass

5 yds./plus loss of down

One hand waved behind back
followed by loss of down
signal. pg.48

MAKE THE CALL!
Penalty?

Intentional grounding of pass

10 yds./plus loss of down

Parallel arms waved in
diagonal plane across body,
followed by loss of down
signal. pg.48

MAKE THE CALL!
Penalty?

Interference with forward pass or fair catch.

Pass- The ball is placed at spot of the foul.
Fair catch- 15 yds. against offending team.

Hands open and extended forward from shoulders with hands vertical.

MAKE THE CALL!
Penalty?

Invalid fair catch signal

5 yds.

One hand waved above the head.

MAKE THE CALL!
Penalty?

Ineligible receiver or ineligible member of kicking team downfield

10 yds.

Right hand touching top of cap.

MAKE THE CALL!
Penalty?

Illegal contact

10 yds.

One open hand extended forward.

MAKE THE CALL!
Penalty?

Offside, encroachment or neutral zone infraction

5 yds.

Hands on hips.

MAKE THE CALL!
Penalty?

Illegal motion at snap

5 yds.

Horizontal arc with one hand.

MAKE THE CALL!
Penalty?

Loss of down, associated with intentional grounding-10 yds. illegal forward pass-5 yds.

Both hands behind head.

MAKE THE CALL!
Penalty?

Interlocking interference, pushing or helping runner

10 yds.

Pushing movement of hands to front with arms pointed downward.

MAKE THE CALL!
Penalty?

Personal foul

15 yds.

One wrist striking the other above head.

MAKE THE CALL!
Penalty?

Unsportsmanlike conduct.

May result in penalty yardage or ejection from the game.

Arms outstretched palms down.

MAKE THE CALL!
Penalty?

Illegal cut Illegal block
below the waist

15 yds.

One hand striking front of thigh,
preceded by personal foul signal.
pg.52

MAKE THE CALL!
Penalty?

Illegal cut Chop block

15 yds.

Both hands striking side of thighs, preceded by personal foul signal. pg.52

MAKE THE CALL!
Penalty?

Illegal cut Clipping

15 yds.

One hand striking back of calf,
preceded by personal foul signal.
pg.52

MAKE THE CALL!
Penalty?

Illegal crackback

15 yds.

Strike of an open hand against the mid-thigh, preceded by personal foul signal. pg.52

MAKE THE CALL!
Penalty?

Player disqualified

Ejection signal, pumping fist with raised thumb.

MAKE THE CALL!
Penalty?

Tripping

15 yds.

Repeated action of right foot on back of left heel.

MAKE THE CALL!
Penalty?

Uncatchable forward pass

Palm of right hand held parallel to ground above head and moved back and forth.

MAKE THE CALL!
Penalty?

Twelve men in offensive huddle
or too many men on the field

15 yds.

Both hands on top of head.

MAKE THE CALL!
Penalty?

Safety

Palms together above head, 2 pts. awarded to defensive team, offensive team kicks from 20 yard line.

MAKE THE CALL!
Penalty?

Touchdown, field goal or successful try.

Both arms extended above head.

MAKE THE CALL!
Preceeded by time out signal.
Penalty?

Touchback

Hands crisscrossed above head followed by arm swung at side.

Preceded by time out signal. pg.17
MAKE THE CALL!
Penalty?

Referee's timeout

Time out signal followed by one hand placed on top of cap.

MAKE THE CALL!
Penalty?

Reset playclock—25 seconds

Pump one arm vertically.

MAKE THE CALL!
Penalty?

Reset playclock—40 seconds

Pump two arms vertically.

MAKE THE CALL!
Penalty?

Fourth down.

One hand above head
with a closed fist.

MAKE THE CALL!
Penalty?

Spearing with helmet

15 yds.

Fist pointed to side of head,
preceded by personal foul signal.
pg.52

SECOND HALF

It's time to play the second half with <u>you</u> as the referee.

Select someone to announce the 'call'.

Now it is up to you to demonstrate the correct signal and announce the correct penalty yardage for each call.

Score (1) point for every correct signal and (1) point for every correct penalty assessment.

Have some fun with your friends and family by making a game of it.

We have provided the following rating system, but feel free and creative to assign your own description for degrees of expertise.

<u>Referee rating system</u>

86-91	Superbowl referee.
71-85	Playoff referee.
51-70	Regular season referee
31-50	College referee.
16-30	High school referee.
0-15	You are definitely a newbie.

Referee's Challenge. Part 1
Rate your skills on page 87.

pg.	Have someone announce the call	Signal the action

3   Crowd noise, dead ball or neutral zone.

5   Delay of game.

7   Facemask.

9   False start, illegal formation, kick/or player out of bounds.

11   Ball illegally touched, kicked or batted.

13   Time out.

15   No timeout, time in with whistle.

17   First down.

19   Illegal touching a forward pass/kick.

21   Holding.

23   Illegal shift.

25   Illegal use of hands, arms or body.

27   Penalty refused, incomplete pass, missed field, extra point or play over.

29   Pass juggled inbounds/caught out of bounds.

31   Illegal forward pass.

33   Intentional grounding of pass.

35   Interference with forward pass or fair catch.

37   Invalid fair catch.

39   Ineligible receiver or member of kicking team downfield.

41   Illegal contact.

43   Offside, encroachment or neutral zone infraction.

Referee's Challenge. Part 2

OVERTIME!

Referee's advanced skill level questions

If you found the 'Referee's Challenge' too easy and was no match for your knowledge and expertise of the gridiron then read on Mr. Expert and see how you fare in overtime.

Here are 12 questions for all the experts to contemplate.
The answers and references begin on the next page.
If you are really the expert you think yourself to be then don't hurry to flip over to the answers on page 92.

1. How many (5) yard penalties can you name?

2. How many (5) yard penalties are there?

3. How many (10) yard penalties can you name?

4. How many (10) yard penalties are there?

5. How many (15) yard penalties can you name?

6. How many (15) yard penalties are there?

7. Name the two 'combination' penalties and both penalties applied.

8. What penalty is given if a team arrives late on the field prior to scheduled kickoff?

9. There are nine (9) defensive fouls which do not necessarily give the offensive team an automatic first down. How many can you name?

10. What happens if a player/person comes on to the field and tackles a runner apparently en route to a touchdown?

11. What is the penalty for using a helmet (not worn) as a weapon?

12. There are eight (8) '15 yard' penalties which may disqualify a player (if deemed flagrant). How many can you name?

Answers to "Referee's advanced skill level questions"
Summary of penalties reference is provided on pages 93 thru 95.

Questions 1-2 There are 32 (5) yard penalties. pg.93

Questions 3-4 There are 7 (10) yard penalties. pg.94

Questions 5-6 There are 19 (15) yard penalties. pg.94

Question 7 pg.94

1. A forward pass thrown from beyond the line of scrimmage.
2. Intentional grounding of a forward pass (safety awarded if passer is in own end zone).
   If foul occurs more than 10 yards behind line, play results in loss of down at spot of foul.

Question 8   (15) yards and loss of coin toss option. pg.94

Question 9   (1)Offside,(2)encroachment,(3)delayofgame,(4)illegalsubstitution, (5)excessive timeouts, (6)incidental grasp of facemask, (7)neutral zone infraction,(8)running into the kicker, (9)more than 11 players on the field at the snap. pg.93

Question 10   A touchdown is awarded when the referee determines a palpably unfair act deprived a team of a touchdown. pg.95

Question 11   15 yards and automatic disqualification. pg.95

Question 12 pg.94

1. Striking opponent with fist.
2. Kicking or kneeing opponent.
3. Striking opponent on head or neck with forearm, elbow, or hands whether or not the initial contact is made below the neck area.
4. Roughing the kicker.
5. Roughing the passer.
6. Malicious unnecessary roughness.
7. Unsportsmanlike conduct.
8. Evident unfair act. (Distance penalty determined by the referee after consultation with other officials.)

Summary of penalties

In the effort to provide this completed compilation of call signals and penalty assessments several resources and references were obtained for accuracy.

Automatic First Down
1. Awarded to offensive team on all defensive fouls with these exceptions:

(a) Offside.
(b) Encroachment.
(c) Delay of game.
(d) Illegal substitution.
(e) Excessive time out(s).
(f) Incidental grasp of facemask.
(g) Neutral zone infraction.
(h) Running into the kicker.
(i) More than 11 players on the field at the snap.

Five Yards

1. Defensive holding or illegal use of hands (automatic first down).
2. Delay of game on offense or defense.
3. Delay of kickoff.
4. Encroachment.
5. Excessive time out(s).
6. False start.
7. Illegal formation.
8. Illegal shift.
9. Illegal motion.
10. Illegal substitution.
11. First onside kickoff out of bounds between goal lines and untouched or last touched by kicker.
12. Invalid fair catch signal.
13. More than 11 players on the field at snap for either team.
14. Less than seven men on offensive line at snap.
15. Offside.
16. Failure to pause one second after shift or huddle.
17. Running into kicker.
18. More than one man in motion at snap.
19. Grasping facemask of the ball carrier or quarterback.
20. Player out of bounds at snap.
21. Ineligible member(s) of kicking team going beyond line of scrimmage before ball is kicked.
22. Illegal return.
23. Failure to report change of eligibility.
24. Neutral zone infraction.
25. Loss of team time out(s) or five-yard penalty on the defense for excessive crowd noise.
26. Ineligible player downfield during passing down.
27. Second forward pass behind the line.
28. Forward pass is first touched by eligible receiver who has gone out of bounds and returned.
29. Forward pass touches or is caught by an ineligible receiver on or behind line.
30. Forward pass thrown from behind line of scrimmage after ball once crossed the line.
31. Kicking team player voluntarily out of bounds during a punt.
32. Twelve (12) men in the huddle.

10 Yards

1. Offensive pass interference.
2. Holding, illegal use of hands, arms, or body by offense.
3. Tripping by a member of either team.
4. Helping the runner.
5. Deliberately batting or punching a loose ball.
6. Deliberately kicking a loose ball.
7. Illegal block above the waist.

15 Yards

1. Chop block.
2. Clipping below the waist.
3. Fair catch interference.
4. Illegal crackback block by offense.
5. Piling on.
6. Roughing the kicker.
7. Roughing the passer.
8. Twisting, turning, or pulling an opponent by the facemask.
9. Unnecessary roughness.
10. Unsportsmanlike conduct.
11. Delay of game at start of either half.
12. Illegal low block.
13. A tackler using his helmet to butt, spear, or ram an opponent.
14. Any player who uses the top of his helmet unnecessarily.
15. A punter, placekicker, or holder who simulates being roughed by a defensive player.
16. Leaping.
17. Leverage.
18. Any player who removes his helmet after a play while on the field.
19. Taunting.

Five Yards and Loss of Down (Combination Penalty)

1. Forward pass thrown from beyond line of scrimmage.

10 Yards and Loss of Down (Combination Penalty)

1. Intentional grounding of forward pass (safety if passer is in own end zone). If foul occurs more than 10 yards behind line, play results in loss of down at spot of foul.

15 Yards and Loss of Coin Toss Option

1. Team's late arrival on the field prior to scheduled kickoff.
2. Captains not appearing for coin toss.

15 Yards (and disqualification if flagrant)

1. Striking opponent with fist.
2. Kicking or kneeing opponent.
3. Striking opponent on head or neck with forearm, elbow, or hands whether or not the initial contact is made below the neck area.
4. Roughing kicker.
5. Roughing passer.
6. Malicious unnecessary roughness.
7. Unsportsmanlike conduct.
8. Palpably unfair act. (Distance penalty determined by the Referee after consultation with other officials.)

15 Yards and Automatic Disqualification

1. Using a helmet (not worn) as a weapon.
2. Striking or purposely shoving a game official.

Suspension From Game For One Down

1. Illegal equipment. (Player may return after one down when legally equipped.)

Touchdown Awarded (Palpably Unfair Act)

1. When Referee determines a palpably unfair act deprived a team of a touchdown. (Example: Player comes off bench and tackles runner apparently en route to touchdown.)

Index and page reference

ABOUT THE AUTHOR

Rick Yearout lives in Morton, Washington with his wife Ruth where he works as an IT consultant. They are both avid football fans and enjoyed working together on this book. Rick also composed, arranged and recorded an instrumental CD entitled "City to Shore". He has written and recorded several other songs such as "Red, White and Blue," a patriotic tribute to our American servicemen. In his leisure time he relaxes by playing his 12-string guitar.

Made in the USA
Columbia, SC
19 November 2017